Author of Temptations

Poetry Collection
INTO MY GARDEN
Homage to Emily Dickinson

María Palitachi
(Farazdel)

AUTHOR OF TEMPTATIONS

Nueva York Poetry Press LLC
128 Madison Avenue, Suite 2RN
New York, NY 10016, USA
+1(929)354-7778
nuevayork.poetrypress@gmail.com
www.nuevayorkpoetrypress.com

Author of Temptations
© 2025 María Palitachi (Farazdel)

ISBN-13: 978-1-966772-81-1

© *Into My Garden Collection vol.* 04
(Homage to Emily Dickinson)

© Publisher & Editor-in-Chief:
Marisa Russo

© Blurb:
Marianela Medrano

© Cover Designer:
William Velásquez Vásquez

© Layout Designer:
Agustina Andrade

© Author Photograph:
Palitachi@me.com

© Cover Artist:
Andy Moreta S.
andy@pixeltweaker.com

Palitachi, María
Author of Temptations / María Palitachi. 1ª ed. New York: Nueva York Poetry Press, 2025
132 pp. 5.25" x 8".

1. Dominican Poetry   2. Latinx Poetry   3. Hispanic American Poetry.

All rights reserved. No part of this publication may be reproduced, distributed, or transmitted in any form or by any means, including photocopying, recording, or other electronic or mechanical methods, without the prior written permission of the publisher and the author except in the case of brief quotations embodied in critical reviews and certain other noncommercial uses permitted by copyright law. For permissions contact the publisher at: nuevayork.poetrypress@gmail.com.

*Love is so startling it leaves little time for anything else.
Morning without you is a dwindled dawn.*

EMILY DICKINSON

Author of Temptations is dedicated to all the silent kisses turned into the best possible lover one can ask for during the silver years.

Now that we found each other again under stricken circumstances let's not waste any more time negating the sweet passion the universe has return to us.

Let's hope we can do justice to the lost time the route imposed upon us.

I repeat with all my heart Barry White's lyrics: *I never going to give you up again. I am going to stay right here with you.*

I

The Perks of passion

AUTHOR OF TEMPTATION

I

In the depths of time,
where embers glow,
a passion reawakens
after decades' flows.

One soul and another,
once entwined,
now fate's paths collide,
desires unconfined.

Times may have passed
like whispers in the wind,
but their flame of attraction
refused to rescind.

Destiny's dance
led them back to embrace,
a passion long dormant,
now eager to retrace.

Their eyes locked
each other on a city corner,
igniting a flame,
memories bittersweet.

No one to blame
but the impatience of youth—
their longing rekindled,
now revealed in truth.

II

Aching hearts awakened,
as time melted away,
their souls rekindled
in a passionate display.

The moments they missed,
the years spent apart,
turned mere echoes
in the beating of their hearts.

In clandestine rendezvous,
they found solace and bliss,
a forbidden affair,
a stolen kiss.

They savored stolen glances
in the moon's gentle light,
creating a world

where their love could take flight.

Whispered secrets shared,
in the secret of the night,
an affair of passion,
burning wild.

With every stolen touch,
their hearts would soar,
and their love, like a wildfire,
could be ignored no more.

No regrets for the past
or a future unknown.

In this affair of passion,
they were finally home.

THE ENDLESS KISS

One more for the road,
traveling within wherever one goes—
the Sensei of it all.

A testament lingers,
repeating thousand times
on millennium lips,
making its mark
with a uniquely captive tongue.

IMPLANTED ON YOU

I go around licking,
smelling each drop spilled from your soul.

And around, I absorb each tear
that beats in your absence.

I hold your name under my tongue
while the fins of a fish
walk like an army of ants,
building memoires.

The feeling of the first kiss—
you took from me,
or I drank from you—
comes back,
while far away, you're doing the same.

To think of the past for a second
is to relive an eternity in you.

PRELUDE TO MAY EIGHT-TEEN

Kisses have no company
The smooches are lonely.

Without your lips, they fall apart,
dry, bending like a flower
in the desert—no wind to touch,
no breeze to spread their fragrance,
in need of the softness,
the care of your hands
to bring them back to life.

Hurry like a hurricane
with the speed of a turtle.
Mimic the strength of the ocean,
never tiring of splashing the shore.

So, hurry, sweetheart. Sleep tight
and dream of the best possible existence,
as you open your eyes on a bed
that tastes like my sweet lake.
Let the distance fail as twist,
self-synchronizing our bodies into one.

The ritual of kisses pound over bongos,
and the stick grows strong,
bouncing on small rocks.

Let's embrace it like a shadow
covering the earth on a cloudy day.

Allow myself to melt on you,
wetting your salty neck
on a body of love,
while the forever spring of Rodin
dwells here with us.

So, hurry, my darling,
before the light gives away
our flourishing love to others.

Concoction

Drifting closer
is drifting away from the self.
A love that rerouted itself
after forty-plus years—
two marriages:
one ending in divorce with a child,
the other, a widower mourning a lost.
Without searching,
the heartbeat found each other
again and again,
never letting go.

The Rain

The rain and I wandered,
Drawn by the scent of your absence-
with search the silence,
each drop falling
with the longing I carried,
both of us aching
to touch your skin
for the same reason.

Invisible

Through an anonymous lens,
he left few kisses
and a wet spot…

Love is a losing game.
After all, I'd rather walk alone,
but love won't let me.

Passionate

Love is spoken here incognito,
sin after sin,
lip to lip,
body to body,

sparks to heaven
quietly.

II

The exile of the body

When I met you, I loved you.
Now I pity you.
LOUISE GLÜCK

TWO LOVERS TRAPPED

I

Two lovers, bound by vows,
unfulfilled promises,
trapped in lives
slowly fading into shadow.
Their hearts intertwined—
a love they couldn't deny,
yet destiny placed them
behind separate doors.

II

The Secret Flame
They sought warmth
in cold marriages,
craving a connection
deeper than duty.
The passion was gone,
but the chains remained.
In secret, they met—
moments stolen,
ecstasy blooming
in a forbidden garden.

III

The Impossible Dream
Torn between desire and burden,
they lived inside a wildfire.
Dreamt of distant shores
where they could be free,
but reality,
always cruel,
kept their love
buried deep.

IV

The Turning Point
Years passed.
The flame flickered—
sometimes shameful,
always real.
And then,
fate intervened.
One door opened,
and they stepped through.

V

Freedom and Judgment
They broke their silence,
shattered their pasts,
risked it all—
for love.
Their old lives crumbled.
Judgment came,
but hand in hand,
they stood firm.

VI

Love Fulfilled
In each other's arms,
peace returned.
The pain,
released.
No longer hidden.
No longer trapped.
Love, at last,
unbound.
What was meant to be,
now finally is.

PERFIDY

In the shadows of forbidden desire,
lies a tale of passion, veiled in fire.

Infidelity's secret, a complex dance,
where hearts entangled take a chance.

Whispers exchanged beneath
    the moon's glow,
a clandestine affair few will ever know.

In stolen glances and lingering touch,
a secret passion burns, craving much.

Behind closed doors, a world unfolds,
where loyalty's bonds begin molds.
But within the depths of hidden sin,
the heart wrestles with a turmoil within.

For infidelity's secret passion rides,
on waves of guilt, where love collides.

A web of deceit spun with a thread,
as promises to unravel, trust left in shreds.

During this tangled affair,
there's a hunger for love that's still there.

Forbidden love's flame can't be denied,
though it leads down a treacherous ride.

The intensity of stolen caress,
in the arms of another, emotions undress.

A secret liaison in the dead of night,
a paradoxical blend of wrong and right.

Infidelity's passion is a dangerous game,
leaving hearts battered, scarred with shame.

Yet for some
It's a path they choose to take,
leaving lives shattered in its wake.

So let me ponder the depths of this affair—
a tale of passion, desire, and despair.

Remember dear heart,
the price it demands,
for secrets of infidelity
leave no one with clean hands.

THE REGRETS OF INFIDELITY

Shadows cast upon the heart,
A tale of regrets torn apart.

Infidelity, a painful sting,
leaving scars that forever cling.

In moments of weakness, temptations lure,
Fidelity's bond, it did obscure.

A choice made in a moment's bliss,
unaware of the pain it would enlist.

The regrets now weigh heavy and deep,
a shattered trust, a love to keep.
The guilt consumes, like a burning flame,
haunting whispers, echoing shame.

The ache of a heart once true,
now tainted by actions it can't undo.
Betrayal's price, a heavy toll—
a broken bond, the eternal soul.

In the darkness, a glimmer of light,
a chance to mend, to make things right.
With honesty and remorse, a path to seek,
Redemption's hope for the hearts that weep.

For infidelity brings lessons learned:
to cherish love, not let it be spurned.
To value trust, to hold it dear,
and let regrets guide us to a future clear.

So, let us learn from the pain we've known,
to nurture love, to not be prone.
For in the depths of remorse's abyss,
lies the potential for a love that persists.

THE SORROWS OF A WANTED LOVE

A clandestine affair lays the tale
of a mistress, burdened with despair.

A woman desired, yet forever concealed,
her sorrows, a secret, she's forced to shield.
Her destiny is entwined in a complex maze,
her presence must remain a hidden gaze.

Yearning for love, yet never allowed,
her heart enthralling, her voice disavowed.

She longs for a love she cannot chase,
her freedom undone, a forbidden embrace.
A wanted mistress, forever on the run,
in a world where her existence fades, known.

SECRET LOVE AFFAIR

In the shadows of night,
a secret love affair
unfolds within two souls
consumed by a dare.

Love,
a hidden flame,
forbidden and wild,
fueled by stolen moments.
They find their escape
in the depths of secrecy,
a world of their own,
where desires take shape.
But love must remain hidden,
bound by secret's heavy chain.

Their hearts locked away,
in the depths of underground desire.

True Incognito

In the quiet corners
of a seemingly typical life,
a lover lived with a secret,
concealed from his partner's sight.

For within his heart,
a flame burned bright,
his true darling from youth
hidden from the light—
a love he could never subdue.

The anchor he lives with,
oblivious to his heart's affair,
unaware of the longing,
the depth of his despair.

Their weeks were filled with routines,
passion growing thin,
while his heart yearned for a "Brown skin",
a destiny he couldn't rescind.

They met decades ago,
a love that sparked with fire,
their souls intertwined,
their passion reaching higher.

But circumstances
had torn them apart—
a cruel twist of fate.
Now they both lived a double life,
a love they couldn't sate.

Every stolen moment,
every secret rendezvous,
filled their heart with guilt,
but also, with growing affection.

He found solace in her arms,
his true love's embrace,
a forbidden affair,
a love he couldn't erase.

He lived with the other woman,
her facade carefully maintained,
yet his heart belonged elsewhere,
to a love that remained.

He wondered
if she ever suspected the truth—
the depth of his deception,
the ache from his youth.

For in the end,
true love cannot be denied.
    Infraganti…

The In-Between

Without your trace
I am a comatose parasite.

My system is choking with passion,
a poet who migrates every word,
climbing a ladder
to acquire your soul.

While hope was missing,
lost in oblivion,
our life had no room
to become anything else.

Captivity

In captivity
affection sprouts
from a shadow.

III

Testament of time

LOVE, A LIMITED EDITION

Love, a limited edition,
rare and divine,
a treasure so precious,
impossible to define.

It knows no boundaries,
no limits to reach,
a feeling that transcends
what words can teach.
Like a fleeting moment,
it blooms and fades,
a delicate dance
that time swiftly evades.

In the vast universe,
it's a shooting star,
leaving a trail of magic,
felt near and far.
A precious gem,
cherished and adored—
not something to be taken
lightly, ignored.

It's a symphony of emotions,
a melody in the air,
a painting of colors
that hearts forever share.
Sometimes, it's a whisper,
a gentle touch,
a sweet caress
that makes hearts clutch.

Other times, it's a storm,
wild and fierce,
a passion that burns,
unyielding, clear.

Love, a limited edition,
not easily found—
but when discovered,
it spreads all around.

It's a secret language,
understood by few,

a deep connection,
like butterfly wings,
delicate, rare.

It brings light to darkness,
hope to despair.

Love, a limited edition,
yet infinite in its grace,
a gift, a reminder
that hearts are forever enchanted.

So let us treasure love,
in its rare form.

Famine

I

For decades, love wrapped bubble blanket,
lost at sea like a message in a bottle,
yearning to be rescued,
to be restored to its original form—
to return and love.
as if it had never been lost.

II

The heart, a specialist
at enduring pain,
suffers quietly,
day by day.

The aches worship hope and honey
while famine nests like a long shadow.

Now, it is a living body,
like any other organism,
digging deeper into the soul.
Love bleeds into itself,
drifting far from fears.

Is it countless?

I

What good is it to love back?
What good is it to adore so many lovers?
They will never have my eyes.

II

In the scribble of each lip,
an exotic light is reborn.
It runs along a tongue,
which we are within.

III

An animal is on the loose,
living in a fleeing world.
It is called love.

(They called it love)
Then…
>   it must be love.

Rendezvous

With Rodin as the forever spring,
spurting over the body,
making it younger, less confused.
A half-life of a stolen heart hang,
like a marionette awaiting
no more crafting.
I wait for the next one,
still swooning from the last kiss.

EYEWITNESS

Your absence makes me invisible
to any possible light that can penetrate
my ebony skin.

Before your lips sealed your love on me,
I felt it through the windows
of your senses and soul.

A careless spirit tattoos our skin,
like the lipstick between the distance
of my lips and your T-Shirt.

Death and Silence

When no one mentions our names,
I will be with you.

Age doesn't stand a chance with us.
My heart always had you as its owner,
even if neither of us realized it.

GETTING OLD WITH US

If I were to play an instrument,
let it be your body—
its notes already written
on my hands.
I'm not saying come over,
but I'll be here,
burning,
ready
to compose pleasure into you.

I place a feather
on every kiss you exhale,
so they can find their way back
when silence cloaks you—
invisible,
driving nowhere,
your kiss still soft
on my lips.
On a single grain of rice,
the earth etched our story.

Only we
can live it,
taste by taste—
each grain a vow
to grow old
together.

IMPLANTED ON (UNFOLDED)

I still taste the things that spill out of you
not just your tears, but the silence too.
That deep kind of quiet that lingers after
words fall away. There's salt in it.
And something that might be love,
or its echo.

Your absence hums in the spaces you used
to fill.
Your tears — I can feel them still —
soft, like a heartbeat
where you used to be.
I carry your name in my mouth,
tucked just beneath my tongue
where it stays warm,
anyplace it waits.

I think of fish drifting slowly in the dark,
mindless but deliberate —
like ants building something
out of instinct.

Like how we build memories
out of nothing but time and repetition.
That first kiss —
I still don't know if you gave it
or if I took it.
Either way,
it's still burning through me,
like it just happened.
You're far from me now.
But I feel it —
some part of you doing the same.
Maybe remembering.
And maybe that's all remembering is —
returning.

IV

The turning point

THE KISS COLLECTOR

The engineer of a kiss,
its construction time for invasion.
To master the art of kissing,
an ongoing practice,
manipulated by a three-inch tonged,
zigzagging in precision.

The collector's tattoos kisses
on a cherry tree,
saving them from the touch of birds
who sing fertility,
an incognito symbol of humanity.

The kisser collector revels in the harvest,
savoring the squeeze of lips,
a contrast to medieval times,
caught in a tongue twister.

Occasionally,
a mercenary of statues caught in stillness.
While jasmine vines embrace themselves,
ready for the next collection of kisses.

THE OTHER KISS

Within the realm of a kiss's touch lies
an unknown world,
a feeling indescribable.
The inside of a kiss, so divine,
where hearts intertwine, souls align.

It's a language spoken without any sound,
a symphony of emotions
that knows no bound.
In that moment, time stands still,
as lips meet, a connection to fulfill.

The inside of a kiss holds untold secrets,
a story of passion, a tale to unfold.
It speaks of desire, longing, and bliss—
a gateway to a world lovers can't miss.

In the depths of a kiss,
a universe uncharted
where dreams and fantasies
have long departed.

A sanctuary of love, a sacred space,
where two souls find solace
in a sweet embrace.

In its gentle touch, love's essence resides,
a magical journey where hearts collide.
So let us cherish the inside of a kiss,
for it's a gateway to a world of eternal bliss.

The Shadow of Love

In twilight's realm, where shadows dance
with gentle grace, and hearts take a chance
lies the essence of love, elusive and free—
a captivating enigma that none could foresee.

In the depths of darkness, love finds its way,
casting its spell with a subtle display.

A silhouette of emotions, unspoken and deep,
where secrets reside, in shadows they creep.

The shadow of love, a mystical veil,
shrouding hearts in a tender travail.
It whispers in echoes, like a silence song,
a language unspoken, but ever so strong.

Like a full moon night, love's shadow appears,
caressing the soul, erasing all fears.
It lingers in moments, fleeting and brief,
leaving traces of passion, a bittersweet relief.

In the shadows, love's secrets unfold,
where vulnerability and desires behold.
It hides from the world, a clandestine affair,
leaving hearts in longing, in whispered prayer.

But do not the fear the shadows' embrace,
for light can still find its place,
guiding us to love that's right,
ever in the darkest night.

So let us cherish the shadow's allure,
for within its depths, love's journey is pure.
In darkness, love's essence will always lie—
a testament to the attraction
that will never die.

BRAILLE

The lamps dimmed,
went eyeless—
in silent reverence
for the blindfolded.
They erased the Phantom
stroke by stroke,
until he became
only a ghost.

THE ALPHA KISS

A silent alphabet in bliss,
passion woven inside the thief of time.

The act of love,
a forever dance in the mud,
to reinvent what love can be.

V

The impossible still burns

(Im)Possible Love

In the kingdom of dreams,
hope takes a flight,
lies the tale of an impossible love,
shining bright.
Two souls, destined to be worlds apart,
yet their hearts entwined,
forever from the start.

Like the sun and moon, they never collide,
yet in their distance, a love does reside.
They yearn for each other, across vast divide,
a love that's forbidden, impossible to hide.

Their paths, like parallel lines,
never to meet,
but their souls,
in secret, forever entreat.

Every stolen glance, a momentary bliss,
a love that defies logic, a sweet abyss.

In the depths of their hearts,
a longing so deep,
a love that's forbidden,
yet they dare to keep.

They tread on the edge
of a precipice unknown,
for their love, like a wildflower,
has quietly grown,
and brightly shown.

The world may scoff,
and say it cannot be,
but love knows no boundaries,
no rules or decree.
They cherish their moments,
though fleeting they may be,
a stolen touch,
a whispered word, a love set free.

Through the night,
they find solace in dreams,
where their love can flourish,
like sunlight beams.

In the shadows,
they embrace, hearts intertwined—
an impossible love,
yet they remain resigned.

For even if their love
can never be whole,
in their hearts,
a flame burns,
forever untold.

They hold onto the hope,
that someday, somewhere,
their impossible love
will find a way, somehow.

So, they dance in March's moonlight,
their hearts ablaze—
a love that defies logic,
in a world filled with haze.
An impossible love,
destined to forever yearn,
yet they hold onto the embers,
forever to burn.

Two ex-reunite

In the realm of dreams,
where hope takes a flight,
lies the tale of an impossible love,
shining bright.

Two souls,
destined not to be,
ecospheres apart,
still their moods entwined,
forever to return.

Like a start and swoon,
they never collide,
yet in their distance,
a love does reside.

They yearn for each other,
across vast divide,
a love forbidden,
impossible to hide.

Their tracks,
like parallel streaks,
never to meet,
but their souls,
in secret, forever entreat.

Every stolen glance,
a momentary bliss,
a love that defies logic,
a sweet chasm.

In the depths of their hearts,
a longing so deep,
a forbidden love
they dare to keep.
It treads on the edge
of a precipice unknown,
for their love,
like a wildflower,
has quietly grown.

The world may scoff,
and say it cannot be,

yet their love knows
no boundaries,
no rules or decree.

They cherish every scape—
from the park, the gym, the store—
though fleeting they be,
a stolen touch,
a whispered word,
a love momentarily set free:
in an elevator,
the back of a car,
or while witnessing the waves
kissing the shore.

REVISITED

A bond that withstands,
a love they know they've conquered.
They dance in the shadows,
their love concealed,
in a world where their union
is not revealed,
as the bridge rises.

A secret love affair,
a beautifully hidden art,
their hearts forever entwined,
though kept apart.

THE ESCAPE

Surrounded by wine
and the alphabet of the nights,
a red kiss holds the distance.

Don't run to catch up with me—
I move forward behind you,
walking until sundown.

Walk slowly,
in silence,
and interlock your fingers
between the stars of the road (my hair).

I am closer than you think.
Listen to the violin,
the harp,
breathe in the roses,
taste the gooseberries,
touch the guitar.

In the dreams that dream
Of the bridge of your legs,
And allow the night dew to overflow.

ABYSS

How can one smell love
without craving it?
How to download it
from a dream?

When the juice threatens to end,
we survived on leftovers, warped.

Savage love is the prey,
high season for kisses.
Traffic within the antennas,
yet we remain bottomless.

We become what we survived—
hunters of vanished love.

Momentum

Love has a flawless memory.

It tries to return
to what it once was—
a blind emotion.

ACKNOWLEDGMENTS

Special thanks to friends of many decades, Ann and Patrick Rocco, for making my stay in Pompano Beach better than what I had imagined, great laughs, good cooking and much more...
I also want to thank Cindi Fifer, Marianela Medrano and Marisa Russo for their unconditional time.

ABOUT THE AUTHOR

María Farazdel (Palitachi), Doctor Honoris Causa, endorsed by the University of Monterrey, U.A.O.M., and UNIPEL. She is the author of fifteen poetry books and five Anthologies. Former NYC Assistant Principal. Five times Award Winner Author (AWA). Dominican Medal of Merit, Florida. Medal Icon of Latino American Poetry, SEL, Miami. Member of PEN International, Dominican Republic. In Bolivia she was name Ambassador of Culture by UNESCO 2014 and in Miami 'Ambassador Honorific, by S.I.P.E.A. The Academy of North American Modern Literature New York Chapter named her the International Ambassador of culture. In Granada, Nicaragua 2019 she was named Ambassador International for the Non-Profit USA, Poetry Foundation. Her work is translated in French, Italian, Arabic, Portuguese and Hindi.

TABLE OF CONTENT

Author of Temptations

The Perks of Passion

Author of Temptation · 17
The Endless Kiss · 21
Implanted on You · 22
Prelude to May Eighteen · 23
Concoction · 25
The Rain · 26
Invisible · 27
Passionate · 28

II. The Exile of the Body

Two Lovers Trap · 33
Perfidy · 39
The Regrets of Infidelity · 42
The Sorrows of a Wanted Love · 44
Secret Love Affair · 45
True Incognito · 46
The in-Between · 49
Captivity · 50

III. Testament of Time

Love, A Limited Edition · 53
Famine · 56
Is It Countless? · 57
Rendezvous · 60
Eyewitness · 61
Death and Silence · 62
Getting Old with Us · 63
Implanted On (Unfolded) · 65

IV. The Turning Point

The Kiss Collector · 69
The Other Kiss · 70
The Shadow of Love · 72
Braille · 74
The Alpha Kiss · 75

V. The Impossible Still Burns

(Im)Possible Love · 79
Two Ex-Reunite · 82
Revisited · 85
The Escape · 86
Abyss · 87
Momentum · 88

Acknowledgments · 89
About the Author · 91

INTO MY GARDEN
COLLECTION

English Poetry
Homage to Emily Dickinson

1
September Blue Jays
Hector Geager

2
Embroidery Colony of Love
Maria Palitachi

3
Brain, Heart, and Quantum
Hector Geager

4
Author of Temptations
María Palitachi

OTHER COLLECTIONS

Fiction
INCENDIARY
INCENDIARIO
Homage to Beatriz Guido (Argentina)

Children's Fiction
KNITTING THE ROUND
TEJER LA RONDA
Homage to Gabriela Mistral (Chile)

Drama
MOVING
MUDANZA
Homage to Elena Garro (Mexico)

Essay
SOUTH
SUR
Homage to Victoria Ocampo (Argentina)

Non-Fiction/Other Discourses
BREAK-UP
DESARTICULACIONES
Homage to Sylvia Molloy (Argentina)

OTHER COLLECTIONS

ADJOINING WALL
PARED CONTIGUA
Spaniard Poetry
Homage to María Victoria Atencia (Spain)

BARRACKS
CUARTEL
Poetry Awards
Homage to Clemencia Tariffa (Colombia)

CROSSING WATERS
CRUZANDO EL AGUA
Poetry in Translation (English to Spanish)
Homage to Sylvia Plath (United States)

DREAM EVE
VÍSPERA DEL SUEÑO
Hispanic American Poetry in USA
Homage to Aida Cartagena Portalatin (Dominican Republic)

FIRE'S JOURNEY
TRÁNSITO DE FUEGO
Central American and Mexican Poetry
Homage to Eunice Odio (Costa Rica)

INTO MY GARDEN
English Poetry
Homage to Emily Dickinson (United States)

I SURVIVE
SOBREVIVO
Social Poetry
Homage to Claribel Alegria (Nicaragua)

LIPS ON FIRE
LABIOS EN LLAMAS
Opera Prima
Homage to Lydia Dávila (Ecuador)

LIVE FIRE
VIVO FUEGO
Essential Ibero American Poetry
Homage to Concha Urquiza (Mexico)

FEVERISH MEMORY
MEMORIA DE LA FIEBRE
Feminist Poetry
Homage to Carilda Oliver Labra (Cuba)

REVERSE KINGDOM
REINO DEL REVÉS
Children's Poetry
Homage to María Elena Walsh (Argentina)

STONE OF MADNESS
PIEDRA DE LA LOCURA
Personal Anthologies
Homage to Julia de Burgos (Argentina)

TWENTY FURROWS
VEINTE SURCOS
Collective Works
Homage to Julia de Burgos (Puerto Rico)

WILD MUSEUM
MUSEO SALVAJE
Latin American Poetry
Homage to Olga Orozco (Argentina)

VOICES PROJECT
PROYECTO VOCES
María Farazdel (Palitachi) (Dominican Republic)

For those who think as Emily Dickinson, that: *There is another sky, ever serene and fair, and there is another sunshine, though it be darkness there.* **Author of Temptations** by María Palitachi invites you to come *INTO [HER] GARDEN*. This book was published in July 2025 by Nueva York Poetry Press in the United States of America.

www.ingramcontent.com/pod-product-compliance
Lightning Source LLC
Chambersburg PA
CBHW030315190426
43198CB00051B/695